Coloring.Disney

Fantastic stories occupy the attention of the modern child is not less than the romantic fairy stories of the classic collections. When stories migrate to the screen in the form of cartoons, kids easier to take these stories, they are ready for hours to follow the adventures of favorite characters. Especially since taken a series of many, and inventive multipliers are not going to stop at the achieved level.

Lilo- girl living in Hawaii - the protagonist of this tale. She has no idea how interesting can be everyday earthly life, when it appeared the representatives of alien worlds, albeit small. One such "instance" - Stitch - hits the Earth, and because he has no idea about what you need to behave in accordance with earthly standards and did not destroy, the small but self Lilo has to his re.

Re-Stitch in the end she manages, but there are other mutants, which are now both of them have to deal with. The story is complicated by the fact that the evil alien genetics scientists hunt for scattered through the countries genetic brothers Stitch. Lilo and Stitch have recourse to a wise teacher and together try to thwart the evil plans of geneticists.

Series Heroes periodically enter the various difficult situations. Lilo and Stitch valiantly trying to stop the machinations of evil aliens, and every time they do it. Raising Stitch, Lilo and have to grow up very little, so act responsibly for more "unreasonable" creature. Mysterious aliens, twisted story with an almost detective plot invariably cause delight most children.

In this book you will find the most interesting episodes in the life of the great heroes of the animated series Lilo and Stitch.

Pictures of this animated series are presented in this book in a wide variety.

Coloring Lilo and Stitch More help diversify leisure of your child. Pictures are chosen in such a way that the baby could navigate and find for themselves the most beautiful and attractive. Help your child choose a color to paint pictures. For Lilo as the islanders with tanned skin, you need to choose the appropriate colors. For most newcomers, including Stitch, the main color is blue (cyan), except for the inner surface of the ears, they have series of pink aliens. The images in colorings are fairly simple, so are suitable for employment by even the youngest children. And to clarify selected shades you once again with the baby can be happy to see a good cartoon with dynamic and exciting scenes.

Made in the USA
Lexington, KY
10 December 2016